When Women Rule the World
What Would Change?

Shelley J. Taylor

Printed and Bound in the United States of America

Published and Distributed by:
Professional Publishing House
1425 W. Manchester Ave., Suite B
Los Angeles, California 90047
www.professionalpublishinghouse.com
Drrosie@aol.com
(323) 750-3592

Cover design: Jay De Vance, III

First printing: August 2012
10 9 8 7 6 5 4 3 2 1

ISBN: 978-0-9853259-4-7

DEDICATION

I dedicate this book to all who desire to see the world reach its full potential according to the Creator's plan.

ACKNOWLEDGMENTS

I was given an assignment by the ALMIGHTY, and I am well pleased to have completed my mission. Thank you, Jehovah God, for trusting me with this assignment.

TABLE OF CONTENTS

INTRODUCTION
When Women Rule the World...
What Would Change?

There has been this vision, or story as you will, in my head for over three years. Trying to ignore it would prove to be futile. Many times, I sat down at the computer to start typing, but I failed to come up with only a few words. I begin to tell myself that I am not a writer; therefore, I would ignore the story again. Several months later, the story would creep back into my head. So I signed up for a class at the Lou Walker Senior Center in DeKalb County, Georgia called "Writing My Story." The instructor asked the class to write a story using only *two* words. The words were *"I want."* For some reason, my hand would not stop writing. Those two little words got me started on my quest to writing this story that has been in my head for years.

I understand that this story will be *controversial* to both men and women. However, I must move forward as the messenger of the vision that was placed inside me.

You will find a survey, which was given to 100 women and 100 men, for gathering information and opinions at the end of this story. Keep in mind the question: *What would change?* Let's get started on this journey.

CHAPTER 1

The "Old" World Ruled by Men

(A) Wars; Murders
(B) Animals; Air; Water; Food
(C) Child Molester; Robbery; Gangs; Drug Wars
(D) Domestic Abuse; Racism; Kidnapping; Rape

The "Old" World Ruled by Men

In the beginning, God gave man dominion over Earth. That meant that man had the authority to rule the animals, birds, and the magnificent creatures that swam the oceans. Men were given wisdom and knowledge to keep the air and water pure and clean for his survival. All foods were organic; therefore, man's body was without disease. Jehovah God was so happy with His creation that He took time off to rest on the Sabbath day. He gave his blessings to man, and all the creatures that roamed Earth, flew the skies, and swam the oceans. Then something *terrible* happened, and things *changed.*

Man has truly disappointed God with his given power of dominion over Earth. Our air, food, and waters are so polluted, that it has affected the health of all who inhabits Earth. Let's go deeper to find out why. Chaos is now rampant all over the world. Because of men, we have wars, murders, child molesters, robberies, gangs, drug wars, domestic abuse, racism, rape, kidnapping, and yes, the majority of these crimes are committed by men. I beg the question: when women rule or have dominion over the world, what would change? We'll go deeper into that question shortly.

When I look at the TV show, *America's Most Wanted*, who tops the assailant's list? Men. You say, Shelley, aren't you bashing men? I will say to you, "No, I'm only presenting the truth." I love men; however, I must present the facts in order for me to write my story as the vision was given to me.

Let's look at some facts. Most school shootings are done by boys. Most college shootings are done by young men. There are young boys and men who have been bullied, and came back with a vengeance to shoot everyone in sight. There was a man who entered a courtroom in Georgia and shot the judge, and several other people died because of his rage and bitterness over a woman. Men have bombed buildings in the United States and abroad, and flew airplanes into the Twin Towers in New York City, which is now called 9/11, because it was done on September 11, 2001. Let's go deeper.

(WARS)

Wars have been going on since the beginning of time. Just read the "Old Testament." Has our world ever not had a war going on somewhere? The Vietnam War, World War I, World War II, Iraq, Afghanistan, Korean War, War of 1812, Civil War, the Spanish and Mexican Wars, and the Revolutionary War. These are just some of the wars that come to mind. My God, we have not touched upon all the wars that have happened in Europe, Asia, Middle East and the African continents. Hitler, a man, destroyed over 8 million Jewish people in Germany in World War II. The wars in Africa have destroyed and misplaced an unspeakable amount of people throughout history. Egypt, Israel, and Syria are in chaos and threatening civil wars as of this year 2012. North and South Korea are divided and can go off the handle at any time. Iran, I personally believe, will start the next major war. What are wars about anyway? Greed, power, land, religion, racism, genocide and attitudes of misused words are culprits of many wars. Like Edwin Starr said in his song: "War, what it is good for, Absolutely Nothing!"

(MURDERS)

Murder has become so scary; we lock our doors and windows and hope for the best. It is written in the "Ten Commandments" that "Thou shall not kill," but this commandment has been very much ignored all over the world. Charles Manson, a man, killed Sharon Tate, a movie star who lived in the Hollywood Hills in the 1960s, and is now serving life in prison. Also, men murder their wives and even their children. You say Shelley, women do the same thing and I would say, "You're right." However, men dominate murder on a much larger scale. Anger is so rampant in our society, why? Listen to this story: A 20-year-old male beat his fiancée's 10-month-old baby to death. The man had been playing a violent video game and lost his temper when the baby touched the game's control panel and thus, caused the man to forfeit the game. Change is coming and this will never happen again. You may recall when Jennifer Hudson, a well-known singer, actor, and Academy Award Winner, family was killed. Her mother, brother, and nephew were killed just a few years ago by a jealous and out of control man. There are too many stories like these that are causing our world grief.

(ANIMALS)

When God gave man ruler-ship over the animals, he was to give their existence dignity and respect. Our animals are suffering on a large scale. I must say right now that this will change immediately because animals are my passion. Women will make sure that animals take a priority in this change. Man has caged so many animals out of their natural habitat from the land they use to roam free just so he can make a buck. He has also entombed the magnificent creatures of the ocean into aquariums and water attractions just to make money. Our precious animals are experimented on without any mercy as if they are without feelings. I tell you that animals feel and have emotions, too. That goes for all the fowl in the air and the creatures of the ocean. Animals are experimented on and murdered to the brink of extinction. Many animals are killed just for their tusk, fur, blubber, bones, teeth and skins. God is not happy to see His creations suffering as they do.

(AIR)

The air...what has man done to pollute the air? Greed is a part of that equation. More cars, factories, chemicals known and unknown, sprays, dyes, contaminated landfills, cell phone towers, and satellites hovering over our environment—the air is making people sick! In New York, they discovered a contaminated landfill that caused several high school students to have ticks and muscle spasms. People are unaware of airborne viruses. When I was a young woman living in Los Angeles, California back in the late 80s, it was said we had encountered a fruit fly that would destroy our crops. The government (man) decided to spray a chemical on the entire South Central L.A. (where mostly Black and Hispanic people lived). We could not go outside at a certain time in the evening. The next morning, our cars were covered in soot of whatever chemical they decided to spray. This went on for a couple of months.

Let's not leave out the disaster that happened in Japan last year in March 2011. One of its nuclear plants, built by man, erupted. These plants are so dangerous to mankind. Also, we can never forget the Atomic Bombs in WWII that killed many people and polluted the air. We, the people, suffer with smog, fumes, chemicals—known and unknown—in the precious air we breathe.

(WATER)

Our water has become the dumping ground for many drugs and chemicals. Man has contaminated the waters so bad that people have turned to bottled water. We put filters on our faucets trying to rid our drinking water of chemicals and contaminants. Yes, man was given dominion over water, and that includes the oceans. I'm sad to say that our oceans have had so many oil spills, garbage dumps, waste dumps. This affects the fish we eat from oceans. Many countries around the world have to walk miles just to get clean drinking water. I believe the medications and other contaminants in the water have made people physically and mentally ill. Most of the time, we walk around not knowing why we are in a mental fog. People are quick to anger in this day and age, and I believe it's because of the polluted air and contaminated water. When women rule the world, and they will, within the next several generations to come, our water will be pure. The dominion over Earth by women will come in a later chapter, so get ready and put your seat belts on.

(FOOD)

Oh my God, our food supply is out of control! Yes, we have plenty of food here on the North American Continent, but our sister continents around the world are in dire need. Our food is full of chemicals, known and unknown to the population. It is manmade food. Man has produced food that tastes so good to the population that it is making us sick. This manmade food is so addictive that we need more and more. It has caused us to be fat and overweight. Everything that is boxed, canned, and packaged in our supermarkets has too much sugar, salt, chemicals and dyes to keep the masses of people under control of the government. If you care about your body (God's temple), you will intake pure food and water to sustain your health.

"Getting old does not make you sick, it's getting sick that makes you old," written by Tim Morrow.

Our vegetables and fruits are sprayed with so many chemicals by man, that when it finally reaches our tables, we wonder why we are balding prematurely. Our foods are sprayed and injected with cancer-causing chemicals. What can we do? Become more conscious of what we ingest into our bodies. Read labels, and if you can't pronounce the ingredient, don't eat it. Go to the farmers' markets as much as possible. Grow your own food. Stay away from fast foods as much as possible; they are loaded with known and unknown products. We will talk more about how change will occur when women rule the world in a later chapter.

(CHILD MOLESTER)

This subject is unspeakable. Child molesting is a sick crime that is committed mainly by men. God is truly sad at a child molester. This act is done in the dark. "We all know that what's done in the dark, must come to the light." How a man can molest his own child, is beyond my understanding. Children are kidnapped, molested, and sometimes killed by men. We live in a sinful world, and sometimes the enemy will dominate a particular gender or race.

Man has been dominated by the enemy, which is why our world is polluted and full of crime. This unspeakable act will be swiftly resolved when women rule and have dominion over Earth. Last year in 2011, an eight-year-old boy in New York City begged his mother to let him walk home by himself. The boy just wanted to be a "big boy," and prove he could walk home without his mother holding his hand. With great hesitation, the mother finally agreed to let her child walk home alone. The little boy became the prey to a sick and evil man. The man was caught on camera luring the little boy into his web of destruction. The little boy was killed and now his mother grieves. Unfortunately, this is our world today. Sad, wouldn't you agree?

(ROBBERY)

"Thou shall not steal," is a commandment of God. Yet, man continues to rob banks, homes, stores and people like nobody's business. There was a time when we could leave our front doors unlocked and feel safe in our own homes. Those days are long gone. Men break into homes and take hard-working people's material things. What kind of immoral humans are these? There are even times when a killing might take place in one of the home evasion robberies. Banks are like Fort Knox when you enter them these days. Tellers are protected behind bulletproof glass-walls just in case of a robbery. People's businesses are being robbed all the time. Men go in liquor stores all the time to rob and sometimes kill an innocence person. Some people say we are living in the last days, and we are, the last days of men having ruler-ship over the Earth. Man's last days to rule or have dominion over Earth will end. Ruler-ship or dominion will be given to women in several generations into the future. When that happens, we will have a better Earth. Let's see what else man has done to create chaos.

(GANGS)

Gangs are a way of life in many cities, states, and countries. These cowards are nothing but homegrown terrorists. We've had the mobs of Chicago, New York City, and Miami completely taking over territories by murdering innocent people. Drugs, alcohol, and money are the main culprits for this type of power. Gangs exist because of men. In Los Angeles, the Bloods and Crips are notorious West Coast gangs. Boys and young men have lost their precious lives due to joining these gangs. The Bloods wore red colors, and the Crips wore blue colors. If a young person wore red in the wrong territory, it could mean a good beating or his life…how sad. I knew some of the boys, and they were sweet and kind with no choice but to join a gang or be beaten up. Gangs have so much power over the community, with their drugs and territorial existence that many citizens just looked the other way in order to keep safe in their own homes.

Protection is what a gang provided for some young men, and most were fatherless. My heart went out for many of the boys of Compton, California. I provided them a safe haven inside my home. Many played basketball in the backyard. One evening, we had a drive-by shooting. There must have been ten boys jumping over my fence for safety. I put them in the back den area for their protection. Once again, I must say that all these young lives were boys and young men.

(DRUG WARS)

Drug wars have caused the death of many people around the world. Right now, the Mexican Drug War is causing havoc on the North American states. Understand that money is the root of this evil. Drugs have caused death, imprisonment, and walking zombies all around the world. I've seen relatives, and close friends get trapped by this evil experience. Yes, this is another one of man's way of making money and having power over the weak men, women, and children who have become enslaved by drugs. It has been said that drugs were put into the black community by the CIA (men). Drugs, however, knows no race.

Whites, Blacks, Hispanic and Asians have all been affected by the almighty drug. Movie stars, rock and roll singers have all been affected by drugs. Singers have perished and lost their careers because of drugs. What will women do to change this in the new and upcoming world? We shall find out later.

(DOMESTIC ABUSE)

Domestic abuse has been acceptable here in America and around the world for many generations. It has only been in the last four decades that laws have been implemented to protect women of this ungodly and cowardly act. Men have been abusing women for centuries. Why has this act gone on for so long? The real reasons why men abuse women are because, by nature, women are **NOT** monogamous creatures. Men have threatened, beaten and brainwashed women over the centuries to have only one partner. Yes, I said it. Women are attracted to other men just as well as men are attracted to other women. Men will beat the living daylights out of a woman if she dares to look at another man.

In other countries, women have to cover their hair and sometimes their whole bodies with clothing. Do you think this tradition was implemented by women? Hell no! Over the centuries, women have been brainwashed to suppress their feminine desires of more than one man. Sure, you see the shows on TV showing the man with several wives, but I'm here to set the record straight, once and for all. Women are not monogamous by nature.

Domestic abuse is primarily done by men to show man's power over the woman to keep her in her place. Women have lost their real nature, which has been caused by men and religion over the centuries that many will never reclaim who they really are. They have been taught to be under the submission of man and the teachings of manmade religions. The power, dignity, and the true nature of women will be reclaimed once her awakening begins. This violence has been passed down from generation to generation, and is now embedded in our (women) genes and DNA. Before change can take place, a cleansing of our genes and DNA must take place. I assure you that this will change. Now let's go deeper.

(RACISM)

Racism is a worldwide issue, and has caused, in my opinion, the worst terrorist acts of all mankind. Men had the nerve to go across the Atlantic Ocean and *steal* other human beings from their land. The slave trade was all about money and power. Africans suffered greatly when they were stolen from their land, families, culture, language, religion, stolen name, and most of all their dignity and ways of worshiping their God. Let's not leave out the people from all around the world who suffered by the hand of man. This hate will be dealt with in the coming New World. Our world is full of racism, even in the year 2012. Racism is learned and taught to children, especially among the white race. This evil has spilled over into other races of people who have never hated other people before. Children are not born to hate; they are taught. Men have started wars over racism. Hitler murdered over eight million Jews, because they didn't have blonde hair and blue eyes. Indians in our country barely exist anymore because of their skin color and culture. Man wanted this rich land for himself; therefore, he killed innocent people for land and power.

Racism also comes in the form of women being unfairly paid wages for the same job that men do. Women in a man-dominated workforce can be hell on Earth. Let's take the case of Lilly Ledbetter, a manager for Goodyear Tire Company, who was paid unfair wages by tens of thousands of dollars of her male counterpart manager doing the same work. There are more Lilly's in the workforce than we can believe.

(KIDNAPPING AND RAPE)

Let's see what else man has done to disappoint God. Kidnapping and rape are rampant around the world. Women are kidnapped, raped, drugged, and sold into prostitution against their will at an alarming rate, and not much is done to stop this evil act. Children are kidnapped, raped and killed by men. Young boys and girls are kidnapped and taken to far-off lands in other countries just to satisfy the sexual appetite of men. Men see women as prey for their own sexual appetites and decide to stalk and eventually rape them. These evil violations have left many women scarred for life. Jehovah God use to be pleased when he made man in his own image, now our God weeps with sadness. Look at all the crimes man has committed. Look at the polluted Earth, air, and water. Because of these atrocious crimes, poverty has reaped the four corners of the world. "Enough is enough said God; *"THE LAST DAYS"* have arrived for man to have dominion over my creations. Women will now RULE THE WORLD!"

CHAPTER 2

The "New" World Ruled by Women

(A) Words from the Author
(B) What will Change and How?
    (1) The Mark of the Beast
    (2) The Last Days
(C) Just an F.Y.I. (For Your Information)

The "New" World Ruled by Women

(WORDS FROM THE AUTHOR)

The changing of the guards will start in *the* political arena. The revision of the Constitution, Bill of Rights and all the massive laws will be revised and incorporated by women. The heads of all nations will be governed by women. Her Congress or Parliament will be majority female. All Supreme Courts around the world, which at one time was headed by all men, will consist of a majority of women. Around the world, women will take their places to control a **hurting** world. The right to bear arms will cease to exist. Eliminating wars will be the number one priority women around the world will eliminate. You ask how this will be done. Women will *walk softly but carry a big stick!* Women will go after the manufacturers of weapons and put them out of business. The power of women shall not be underestimated when it comes to eliminating wars. The hand of God will reign for this mission to be carried out. These *Last Days* of men ruling the world is over.

I can hear some men laughing and joking, and even some women saying this author has lost her mind. No such thing can ever happen. Just remember Noah when he was building his Ark and the people didn't believe him when he tried to warn them of the end of time. That's when God sent rain for forty days and forty nights to end a wicked and immoral world, as it was, during that time.

I would think that any person in their right mind would love to live in a war-free world. It will take the power of God to place upon women, to free this world from wars all around the world. Get ready because it is happening, little by little, right before your very eyes every single day. It will not happen overnight, not even in yours or my lifetime, but it will happen.

Remember that women just got the right to vote in 1920 in this country. Now we have more women doctors, lawyers, senators, and women on the *Forbes* billionaire list, women running for president, prime ministers in other nations; we have six women governors in the United States. There are women newscasters, journalists, policewomen, firewomen, college professors, and now women outnumber men in college.

The medical field is forever growing with women, and this is just the tip of the iceberg. At the end of the 1980s, one-third of the doctors graduating from medical schools were women. Women doctors will soon be in the majority in specialties such as obstetrics/gynecology, pediatrics, and psychiatry. They are rapidly making strides into traditionally male territories like surgery and orthopedics. This shift in a now male-dominated profession is changing American medicine. One can already see changes in medical education, as the number of women professors increase in medical schools.

If you don't think women can stop wars, think again my friends. Women are taking their position right before your very eyes. The U.S. Supreme Court was once dominated by all men, now there are three women as of March 2012. Women are taking their places in a hurting world so that change will be for the betterment of all mankind everywhere.

Can you imagine a world with no more wars? Take a moment to think about it. It's hard to do, right? God gave me this vision or message as you will, and now I'm giving it to you. Take it or leave it, but it will happen in the future. The enemy does not want this information to awaken the female/male mind any further; he enjoys conjuring up wars between nations. His purpose is to kill and destroy as many people before the *Last Days* of men end.

As a youngster growing up in the church, I often wondered why the church was full of women and very few men. I remembered when women could not preach or even stand behind the pulpit. Women always had to stand off to the side with a microphone to speak. I was only around ten years old when I was baptized, but I was highly aware of the protocol many churches had when it came to women. Nowadays, women are preachers all over the country, and still growing. Yes, women are taking their places. I promise you that wars will be a thing of the past.

Let's take a moment to recognize some of the women presidents and prime ministers of the 20th and 21st Centuries. I think you will be amazed of the progress women have made at home (U.S.) and abroad.

- **Sirimavo Bandaranaike,** of Sri Lanka (South India), was the first Prime Minister in the world from 1960, 1970 and 1994.

- **Isabel Peron,** of Argentina, was the first woman president in 1974.

- **Indira Gandhi,** of India, was Prime Minister in 1966 and 1980. She was assassinated by her own bodyguards in 1984.

- **Golda Meir,** of Israel, was Prime Minister in 1969.

- **Elisabeth Domitien** was Prime Minister of Central African Republic in 1975.

- **Margaret Thatcher** was Prime Minister of Great Britain in 1979.

- **Maria da Lourdes Pintasilgo was** Prime Minister of Portugal in 1979.

- **Lidia Gueiler Tejada was** Prime Minister of Bolivia in 1979.

- **Dame Eugenia Charles was** Prime Minister of Dominica in 1980.

- **Vigdis Finnbogadottir was** President of Iceland in 1980.

- **Gro Harlem Brundtland** was Prime Minister of Norway in 1981, 1986 and 1990.

- **Milka Planinc was** Federal Prime Minister of Yugoslavia in 1982.

- **Agatha Barbara was** President of Malta (an island in the Mediterranean Sea near Europe and North Africa) in 1982

- **Maria Liberia-Peters was** Prime Minister of Netherlands Antilles in 1984, 1988.

- **Carmen Pereira was** acting President of Guinea Bissau in 1984.

- **Corazon Aquino was** President of Philippines in 1986.

- **Benazir Bhutto was** Prime Minister of Pakistan in 1988 and 1993. She was assassinated in 2007 while campaigning for another term in office.

- **Kazimiera Danuta Prunskiene was** Prime Minister of Lithuania (in Europe) in 1990.

- **Violeta Chamorro was** President of Nicaragua in 1990.

- **Mary Robinson was** President of Ireland in 1990.

- **Ertha Pascal Trouillot was** interim President of Haiti in 1990.

- **Sabine Bergmann-Pohi was** President of German Democratic Republic in 1990.

- **Khaleda Zia was** Prime Minister of Bangladesh in 1991 and 2001.

- **Edith Cresson was** Prime Minister of France in 1991.

- **Agathe Uwillinglyimana was** Prime Minister of Rwanda for nearly a year, and was assassinated by Hutu Soldiers in 1994 during the early days of the Rwanda Genocide.

- **Michelle Bachelet was** President of Chile in 2006.

- **Beatriz Merino was** Prime Minister of Peru in 2003.

- **Yulia Tymoshenko was** Prime Minister of Ukraine in 2005.

- **Micheline Calmy-Rey was** President of Switzerland in 2006.

- **Ellen Johnson-Sirleaf was** President of Liberia in 2006.

- **Han Myung-Sook was** Prime Minister of South Korea in 2006.

- **Portia Simpson Miller was** Prime Minister of Jamaica in 2006.

- **Pratibha Devisingh Patil was** President of India in 2007.

- **Cristina Fernandez de Kirchner was** President of Argentina in 2007.

- **Laura Chinchilla was** President of Costa Rica in 2010.

- **Kamla Persad Bissessar was** Prime Minister of Trinidad and Tobago in 2010.

- **Julia Gillard was** Prime Minister of Australia in 2010.

- **Dilma Rousseff was** President of Brazil in 2010.

- **Yingluck Shinawatra was** Prime Minister of Thailand in 2010.

There are many more women Presidents and Prime Ministers that were not mentioned in this segment. This is just to give my readers a reality check of what's going on around the world with women.

Isabel Peron of Argentina was the world's first woman president. She took office in 1974, becoming the first woman to lead a South American country. Like many other women, who were heads of state, Peron was the wife of a previous president, Juan Peron, and she actually served as vice president during his third term.

When Juan Peron died in office of a heart attack, she assumed the presidency. But unlike Peron's second wife, Eva Peron, who became immortalized by the play "Evita," Isabel Peron, was not popular and she was overthrown by a coup in March 1976.

With all due respect, I must give this lady, my shero, her due respect. **Shirley Anita St. Hill Chisholm** (November 30, 1924-January 1, 2005), was an American politician, educator, and author. She was a Congresswoman, representing New York's 12th Congressional District for seven terms from 1969 to 1983. In 1968, she became the *first African American Woman* elected to Congress. On January 25, 1972, she became the first major-party black candidate for President of the United States, and the first woman to run for Democratic presidential nomination (Margaret Chase Smith had previously run for the Republican presidential nomination). She received 152 first-ballot votes at the 1972 Democratic National Convention.

Preceded by: Edna F. Kelly

Succeeded by: Major R. Owens

Born: November 30, 1924 in Richmond, Virginia

Died: January 1, 2005 (age 80) in Ormond Beach, Florida

Spouse(s):   1) Conrad Chisholm (divorced)

2) Arthur Hardwick Jr. (widowed)

(WHAT WILL CHANGE AND HOW?)

The Mark of the Beast; The Last Days

Since the right to bear arms will cease to exist, **Murders** will be rare. Our society will not be that of utopia, but change incorporated by women will be for the betterment of all mankind. Men, women, and children will be able to walk the streets of this country and other countries without fear of someone with murder on their mind.

There will be no long lengthy trial for the few and rare murders that will happen. Women will deal with murderers swiftly. The guilty will go to prison or face missing limbs, which could be a finger, hand, foot, etc. No limbs, no murders. This will be the *Mark of a Murderer-Beast.*

The right to Bear Arms will only be by those in authority. Men who hunt, will have to check out their raffles with women in charge of the wilderness, and will be under great restrictions to hunt for food only.

In Africa, genocide has damn near destroyed the original man. The murders of men, women, and children in many villages have been nothing but a holocaust. The weapons are usually guns and machetes. Women will rise up and remove these weapons of men who have caused nothing but destruction. Each murderer will have missing limbs; therefore, he or she will no longer be able to murder anyone ever again. This will be *the Mark of the Beast* that they are. They will never have the opportunity to wear prosthesis ever. Many generations will come and go before women completely change our world.

Wisdom, education, and faith in God will be the key to the rise of women all around the world. Change will come. The world cannot continue to function in its current condition. Today many people say we are living in the *Last Days*. I have been hearing this statement since I was ten years old. I'm now sixty-one and have been given what the *Last Days* really mean. Men have had their turn to rule this marvelous creation called earth and have come to the end of their rule. Women are rising up to take their place of dominion to be given by God.

Our animals will no longer be mistreated! Experimentation on animals will be against the law. Anyone caught experimenting on an animal will get the same treatment he or she bestowed upon that creature. All animals will be treated with dignity and respect.

Will we still be able to eat animals? Unfortunately, that will not change. The slaughter of cows, pigs, chickens, goats, lambs, horses, turkeys, dogs, cats and many other creatures will still serve as food to the human race for consumption even when women rule. Mistreatment, such as dog fighting rings, beating animals for no reason, throwing them out of a moving car, kicking them, and starving them to death will end. Mistreatment of animals will be dealt with swiftly. Not only will you serve prison time, but also you will have to serve animals before you are entered back into society. You will serve animals in shelters, kennels or zoos. God made animals before he made man. They were peaceful until man came along and changed their world to a living hell. Animal rights groups around the nation and the world will have more clout when it comes to our animals. Never again will elephants be killed just for their tusk. Deer and bears are killed just to mount on a wall or use as a rug on the floor for show. I'm an animal lover; this change will take place immediately!

Our air/earth is so polluted with chemicals known and unknown to mankind. Because of greed, man has allowed unspeakable pollutants of factories, cars, trucks, buses and insecticides to keep people sick. Cleaner air will be dealt with swiftly. Women will shut down factories that pollute the air. Any car, bus, or trucks that emit smoke will be taken off the streets. Citizens, with proof, will have the opportunity to turn in any perpetrators who violate the act of polluting our earth for compensation. With all the cameras watching you, people will take back our Mother Earth and air. Women will act swiftly on people who pollute the air and Earth.

A special task force will be implemented to watch our roads, and beaches from people who litter. Litter will not be tolerated anymore. Life on this planet will be made more enjoyable and safe for women and their children along with men. *Let's get a clear understanding; men will not lose their place as a man, but rather as a man in control of the planet.* I've heard other people who visit our beaches from the other countries, such as the Caribbean Islands, talk about how dirty our (U.S.) beaches are. They are so right! If you ever visit the islands or the Mediterranean Seas, the waters off the coast of many other countries are blue-green and crystal clear. No longer will our oceans become a dumping ground. Stiff penalties and imprisonment will be put in place. These things will change with the ruler-ship of women.

Our Earth has suffered at the hand of man for an unspeakable amount of time throughout history. Oil spills in our oceans, trees uprooted for no reason. Litter is rampant, and our landfills are filled with items that are not biodegradable. Oil spills will be no more. Women will take their place to make sure spills never happen again to our great and vast oceans. If trees could talk, they would tell you the true history of the world. Trees are alive with oxygen for our human society. Trees are mighty and strong, their roots are vast, their trunks are mighty, and they grow to serve mankind and the animals. Women will take better care of trees. No bulldozer will knock down a tree, especially the all mighty oaks or sequoias just to clear the land for a strip mall. Landfills will be for biodegradable material only. Recycle will be the only way to get rid of old items.

The future will bring forth a better transportation system; therefore, most cars, trucks, and buses that emit pollution in our air will be eliminated. Most major cities will have Metrorails that are so sophisticated that cars may only be used for a Sunday drive, so to speak.

How will women change the world? Little by little, inch by inch, one day at a time. Open your eyes, look and observe, because it is happening at this very moment. This change of man dominance will be hard to imagine and swallow for most. The world cannot, and will not, continue in its present day condition. A change will come only with the help and the authority of God. *This is not my change; I'm just the messenger of the change that's coming.* This change will take several future generations. We will have pure air again, and a cleaner, litter-free Earth.

This garbage we call food will cease to exist in our supermarkets, and shall be replaced with *real food* that nourishes our bodies. The people will start to become sane again in an insane world. We are walking zombies because of dyes and chemicals in our food. Man has made these so-called foods taste so good that our cravings for these unnatural foods have become very addicting. This will change. Such foods that are sold at Famer's Markets will be sold in our supermarkets to nourish our bodies. Billboards and TV commercials of unhealthy foods will banish just like cigarette commercials.

Mothers will breastfeed their babies anywhere of their choosing without remorse from the ignorance of this culture. Breastfeeding is the most natural way of feeding our young, but has been made dirty and turned into a sexual agenda. This will change. Women in other countries can walk around with their breast showing without remorse because it is a natural part of the human body. Man has made the breast of the female into a sexual agenda; therefore, the blindness and ignorance of people in our country have been tainted far too long. The breasts of women are made for feeding our babies. It is time for a new way of thinking and this will happen in the new world.

Women will take their place in providing their children more home cooked meals. The fast-food industry will provide more healthy foods or it shall be shut down. We, the people, will take control over who put what in our foods. I personally miss my Big Mama's homemade ice cream, which was such a special treat. The ice cream in the supermarket is nothing like homemade. I remember going to Ghana, Africa and having a wonderful meal in a restaurant. For dessert, I ordered ice cream. I nearly fell out of my chair. I couldn't believe the pure taste of real cream I had so remembered as a little girl when Big Mama made while sitting on her front porch in Longview, Texas. I caused such a ruckus in the restaurant that all the people in my American group ordered ice cream; they also couldn't believe the real taste of pure ice cream. That was in 2004, and I haven't tasted good ice cream since.

The food in Africa and many other countries I have visited are more pure than our American food. Many foreigners come to America and start their own markets and food industry because they know that our food is full of chemicals. People who come here from the Caribbean Islands and other countries, start losing their hair and getting high blood pressure from our American food. When I went to other countries, I couldn't believe the pure and real taste of the fruits and vegetables. The taste was as I remembered as a little girl. Most of our fruits are tasteless. Man has genetically altered our fruits and vegetables. Women, with the help of God, will change how our food is grown and distributed. We will get back our beautiful skin, eyes, bodies, and hair just by eating nutritional food again. Our sanity depends on it.

The next change will be to eliminate the **Child Molester.** Women and Mothers will not tolerate this unspeakable act, which is mainly committed by men. There will be absolutely no second chances for this horrible crime.

The Surveys, which will be displayed at the end of the book, will show that some surveyors wanted castration immediately bestowed upon the man who commits such a crime. As the messenger of my vision, there will be no castrations of any man. The mark of this beast will be to eliminate his *limbs.* No limbs, no crime. Let's also get an understanding right now. Women, who commit crimes mentioned throughout this book, will be dealt the same punishment as men. Crimes primarily committed by men are the focus of the change that will take place in this hurting world. Anything outside of a crime will be secondary when it comes to change. Our prisons are already overcrowded, and with the *Mark of the Beast* (missing limbs), this will eliminate overcrowding. When this beast walks the streets from now on, children will feel safe knowing that this person, who has no limbs, can't hurt them. Our system of criminal law will be so sophisticated in the future that no innocent man or women will unjustly be marked.

As I write about this horrible crime, the child molester is still dominating the news. Little girls and boys are still being abducted in the year 2012. The first little six-year-old boy that was put on a milk carton, who was abducted back in 1979, is now news headline today. In New York City, the authorities have reopened the case and are now digging in an underground basement for any remains of this child. The parents have kept the same phone number all these years hoping for a phone call from this precious little boy. What a tortuous nightmare many parents have suffered because of these predators. Again, without limbs, these predators will be recognized by the world as the *Mark of the Beast*. Absolutely no second chance is permitted for this unspeakable crime.

What change will take place for robbery? Let's get down to the business at hand very quickly. Without hands or fingers, no robbery can take place. The first time offender's punishment is a missing thumb. The second offense is the other missing thumb.

The third offense is a missing hand. If there is a fourth offense, the other hand will be missing. No limbs, no crime. Society may cringe at the idea of missing limbs at first, but think of it this way—no prison or death penalty has stopped crimes around the world. These crimes still exist and are getting worst. The *Mark of the Beast* is the only thing that will make the world a safer place for the majority of men, women and children. God will give women the highest divine wisdom and knowledge that man took for granted. The world is a mess and change will come. Man had his chance and now women will make the creation of Almighty God safe again for humans, birds, animals, trees, air, and food.

Understand that petty theft is not robbery. Petty theft is like a child or an adult stealing cookies or chips from the store. That is wrong, however, they will not lose any limbs. Strong armed robbery has the intent of hurting or killing people. Women will work out all the details once they are in control.

Gangs/drug wars have terrorized people and their communities for too long. Women would like to send their children to the best schools in safe communities; therefore gangs shall be wiped out completely without mercy in the same manner roaches are eliminated. Gangs will become extinct and a thing of the past. Little by little, people will take back their neighborhoods.

Guns and drugs will be eradicated. Fear that once rocked people will be reversed and felt by gangs. Gangs will now fear the community that will cause the disbursement of this destructive activity at home and around the world. Women raising their children in a safe environment will take priority in a changed world. Whether the female species is in human form, fowl or animal form, she wants to provide a safe environment for her young, and will fight to the death to save them. Get ready world for women to create such an environment. It's been a long time in the making, now a change is going to come.

By law, absentee fathers of boys in gangs will be rounded up and thrown together to give these hurting boys the father figures that's missing in most of these boys' and girls' lives. Yes, I know about these boys because I raised quite a few of them in the city of Compton. Some were worth saving and some were rotten to the core. Love and time with their fathers would make for better young men. Fathers take your position, because women will not raise your children alone anymore! For the fathers who have already stepped up to taking care of their children, this message is not for you. We commend the men who take care of their children. Women who deny fathers from seeing their children will be dealt with swiftly, because it is not healthy for a child not to know both parents. To eliminate gangs, is to eliminate drug wars. Get ready, because change is on the rise.

Domestic abuse/rape and kidnapping will take a turn for the better in this hurting world once women take their place to be in total ruler-ship of the world. Women, children, and some men shall no longer be abused. Again, if you have no limbs, you can't abuse, rape or kidnap anyone. The *Mark of the Beast* (no limbs) will be recognized around the world. Remember I'm only the messenger. If you feel missing limbs are too harsh of a punishment—oh well. Take a look at your local news morning, noon, or night, and then ask yourself who is the main perpetrator of committing these crimes, men or women? Ask yourself, has our world improved or gotten worst?

The rape of women in the military in the United States by men is often swept under the rug. Rape of women in Haiti after the worst earthquake in the Western Hemisphere was out of control. Women were raped during the disaster of Katrina, a hurricane, which leveled homes in Texas, Louisiana, and Mississippi in 2005. So-called refugees that gathered in a large Louisiana dome for shelter is where several women were raped.

I'm so sick of hearing about our little boys and girls being kidnapped, that I can just scream! Children should be able to play outside without fear of some sick man trying to lure them into their car. Most of these children will never see the sight of day light again. There will be absolutely no mercy on the predator that *prey* on children. Again, I must say, "With no limbs there will be no kidnappings, rapes or abuse of any kind."

What will women do to eradicate racism? This will be women's toughest assignment. Only God's wisdom and divine power can show women the steps to take. The *root* of racism is buried so deep in the ground, that it will take a bulldozer to dig it out. Racisms ugly head comes in the form of skin color, gender, your class, your education, the language or dialect you speak, and whether you are a gay man or women, whether you came from the South side or the West side of town. Is my hair Red, Nappy, curly, straight or dread locked. Body shape and size have become the 20th and 21st centuries new racism. Fat is out and skinny is in. We, as women will have our work cut out for us with racism, however God will show us what we need to do, because the power of women alone on this most evil act will take divine intervention.

Bible Prophecy reveals that the present world will be replaced by a new world of God's making. This is what we call the Last Days, but the Last Days of the ruler-ship of man is what this means.

Racism of women on the job has been an evil for many years. Men have been paid more money for the same work that women do, but men get paid more money. That will change in the new world ruled by women. There will be equal pay for equal work.

(JUST AN F.Y.I) For Your Information

It is time for the *awakening* of women so that the world will be a better place to live in. For centuries women have beat themselves up over the infidelity of men. Stop it! Here is why it exists or better yet, this is why men cheat. The enemy of this world has infiltrated man and the white race. Men who have not truly found God will think that it is natural to be non-monogamous. When God gave Moses the "Ten Commandments," *Thou shall not commit Adultery*, for example, he was not just talking to women, but to men also. Therefore, the enemy infiltrated man because of this one commandment to go against God. In other words it's not man's fault for his infidelity, he has been chosen as the dominate species as the assignment of the enemy. The white race has also been chosen as the dominate race to destroy or enslave other races. Some men and women of the white race have finally *awakened* to the fact that the immoral acts they have committed does not come from God.

These acts are so engraved in man and the white race, that they think it is the right way to live. Man thinks he must have more than one woman, when in fact, women feel the same way. Over the centuries, men have brainwashed, beaten, and made women deny their true feminine self. Women can only fantasize of having more than one husband. In the new world, however, men and women will have only one husband or one wife.

The roles of women are changing right before our eyes. Women are becoming airline pilots and men are becoming flight attendants. Women are calling the shots on dating and have become independent when it comes to their money. TV shows like T*he View, The Talk, Wendy Williams Show, Kathie Lee and Hoda, The House Wives of Anything*, is just the tip of the iceberg. Diane Sawyer and Robin Robins have stepped up to be anchor women for the news was real change on TV airwaves concerning women. Like I said before, inch by inch, changes are happening right before our eyes, especially here in North America.

Take a day and really, really watch the world. What do you see when it comes to women? Do you see the roles men play? What does the evening news say about crime and who is committing them? Are you observing how far women have come since the voting rights given to her in 1920? Take one day and really observe, then ask yourself, how long will the world last in its present day condition?

CHAPTER 3

The Surveys

Survey Given by Shelley J. Taylor

This Survey of 100 Men will help me *Write My Story* and you can help.

I have had this story in my Head for about three years. I tried to ignore it, but it won't go away. Sometimes I wake up in the middle of the night thinking about it.

Currently, I signed up for the "Writing My Story" class at the Lou Walker Senior Center to help me get started.

LET'S GET STARTED

THE QUESTION IS:

If Women **Ruled** the World, ***What would Change?***

With all due respect, I only need the question answered with no added criticisms, please.

Name is: ***Optional (Please return within 40 days)***

(Year 2012) 100 Women have already been surveyed.

Return This Page (*in the self-addressed envelope*)

If Women RULED the World, **<u>What would Change?</u>**

_____

_____

_____

_____

_____

_____

_____

_____

_____

_____

_____

_____

_____

_____

_____

_____

_____

SURVEYS BY WOMEN

Written In Their <u>Own</u> Words

13 Surveys

SURVEY #1

Although I think we would still have wars, they would be shorter and few of them. Women think about "others" and see ourselves more as part of a "whole" versus just my "world."

Also, healthcare would be more available and less expensive because focus would be on "care" and not "profitable care"

(No Name)

SURVEY #2

Reflection on the meaning behind the message (change) as for me my lifestyle would (change) and I would gain professional recognition with my new change. And each day we as women would receive inspiration that motivates actions for applying words for women if they ruled the world.

It would take Faith and action, daily inspiration and deed. Change won't be easy. Suggestions, apply it as needed each day to your life for women to rule the world. Change would have to come through Faith and the Creator of this world.

(My Mom, Mary A. Taylor)

SURVEY #3

Healthcare

Healthcare should be provided for everyone, from every economic background. We should provide affordable healthcare, along with skilled physicians. There should be two separate programs:

1. Affordable Healthcare should be provided for citizens of the United States.

2. Affordable Healthcare should be provided for Immigrants, based on their application to become a citizen of the United States.

Operation Incentive

Working as a Section 8 Advisor, for the City of Los Angeles Housing Authority, at least 75% of my caseload could have located a job, or gone to school. Government and State have created county programs, which created a low-income community and state of mind.

I feel people without disabilities, physical/mental, should earn their benefits as follows:

1. Housing
2. Medical
3. Food Stamps
4. Monetary Monthly Payments (AFDC check)

It should be mandatory to learn an occupation and seek employment in their area of training. This will empower our society, giving us a sense of worthiness and responsibility. We need to educate and recondition our communities, by empowering individuals with the necessary tools to be accomplished and productive.

Several prerequisite courses should be provided, before the occupational training can begin:

1. Cultural Sensitivity
2. Sexual Harassment
3. Social Etiquette
4. Professional/Ethical Conduct

Additionally, training should be provided for the following:

1. Reading/Writing
2. Resume and Employment Applications
3. Interviewing Workshop
4. Basic Finance (checking, savings accounts)

(My Sister, Celeste Dixon)

SURVEY #4

Racism...how we treat one another...respect one another... and also the jealousy...envy that we have toward one another...I would eradicate.

Shelley….may you be blessed beyond measure in all of your endeavors….love…and many blessings to you and yours.
(Love Rita, in my camera class)

SURVEY #5

Compassion would be viewed from a different prospective. Details would be induced in everything that's done. Efficient would be a top priority.

(No Name)

SURVEY #6

Yes I think it would be wonderful world women are great and powerful people I wish you lots of succeed.

(No Name)

SURVEY #7

My Opinion: If women ruled the world....... Not that much would change. Behind the scenes Men would still be ruling.

(Maggie)

SURVEY #8

If women ruled the world, children would have absolutely nothing to want for. We would put our little precious darlings first. School systems would be well organized, safe and effective. There would be no hunger. We like to make sure our families are taken care of and fed. The world would be such a beauty because it would reflect us. We would probably be in a bigger debt crisis because most women do not know the value of a budget. The world would be no place like home if it was left up to us women

(Chellie)

SURVEY #9

1. (**Education**) Women have to be better *educated* to have been able to gain the authority to assume leadership roles and earn equitable/higher wages, thus significantly reducing sexism in employment and other areas of society.

2. (**Positions of Authority**) More women would be Presidents, Premiers, Ambassadors, Consulates, doctors/ lawyers Supreme Justices, and other Heads of State just as most societies are headed by men.

3. Women would not be solely dependent on men for their care, well-being and self-esteem.

4. (**Better/Available Health Care**) More focus on women's health: preventative, long-term care and life-threatening.

5. (**Family Planning**) Contraceptives would not be women's near exclusive burden, for more research on men's contraceptives would be forthcoming post haste.

6. (**Sex-based Criminality**) Prostitutes (men and women) and their Johns would be incarcerated, and names would be protected just as Johns' names are. There would be

strict liability for both offending parties.

7. (**Less casual/irresponsible sex...more marriages**) Fewer out-of-wedlock births as men would be required to marry these women or go to jail for a set number of years.

8. (**Protection of Children**) Fewer teen pregnancies as the laws against statutory rape would be strictly enforced (16 & below).

9. (**Better allocation of public funds**) Less proliferation of wars, genocides and other atrocities that consumes funds that assist indigent or needy citizens.

10. (**Strict and speedy punishment of Sexual Predators**) Fewer rapes as the laws against violence would be legislated by women, and carried out swiftly and harshly, including physical and prescriptive castration.

11. (**Significant childcare sharing**) As primary childcare provider Men would take turns caring for the children and other matters around the house and in the relationship, plus spend more time with their in-laws.

12. All States would be community property states so that each party in divorce would be equally situated.

13. Women wouldn't have to worry about their figure so much or their beauty, as they would be the judgers of men.

(Ruby J. Thomas, my camera class)

SURVEY # 10

If women ruled the world, I think that there would be very few changes from culture or the human condition of today. Have we forgotten the hands that rock the cradle rule the world? Women are the source of our current culture because they raise all children. If the house hold is very rich, the children are raised by nannies who are women.

How many women disown the injustice and culpable behavior of the legal system? Are more women against capital punishment than men? I don't think so. Who initiated the "Tea Party" movement? Who bring down Kings, Presidents, CEO'S and the average leader, John Doe? It's women. Are there evidences anywhere that illustrate that if women ruled the world it would be a better place and there would be greater peace in the world? I don't think so. History has proven that women leaders Like Queen Victoria and others were some of the most vicious rulers in their time.

In modern time, since the sixties, here have been tangible evidences that indicated what has happened since women demanded leadership through the women's lib. The cultural change brought about is a mono-sexual population. Men are not different from women in cultural behavior today. All the sexes are the same. Women no longer depend on men and for the most part they have very little respect for the role of a man in the home and in the culture. Women no longer depend on men for procreation. The common practice today is for artificial insemination for procreation and may indulge in same sex relationship. Homosexuality is celebrated today as women are the chief proponent of such behavior. Therefore, I think that if women rule the world, things might be worse than they are today.

(No Name)

SURVEY # 11

Congress would have to pay into social security and Medicare. Laws for equal rights…marriage. Term limits on political office. Get rid of Supreme Court. Universal health care & free choice clinics firm, task masters…get rid of needless laws, but enforce those on the books. Wars would cease to be unwilling to send their sons/daughters into battle.

If women ruled the world, it would be a kinder, gentler place to live. Women would ensure the children would be protected from evil acts, such as, pedophiles, and that there would be mechanism in place to ensure a loving home, food to eat, and educational opportunities for all. If women ruled the world, rape and incest would be crimes punishable by castration. There would be legislation in place to make sure women had control over their bodies…birth control, abortions, etc. would be personal choices. If women ruled the world, war would only exist for reasons of self-defense; there would be no aggressive wars. Problems and conflicts would be resolved through compromise and negotiation. If women ruled the world, people would be allowed to die with dignity. Our environment would be protected from pollution. A cure for cancer would be the top priority and healthy eating would be encouraged in all homes. Chores in the home would be shared equally between men and women. If women ruled the world, it would be mandatory to find something to laugh about each day.

(V. J. Rhodes, in my writing class)

SURVEY #12

If women were in charge of the world, there would be more emphasis on human development in all aspects of our lives. Women have a bias towards sharing resources and finding solutions through cooperation. While I recognize that in some instances women can be very cruel to each other, they tend as a whole to be less violent. Accordingly, national or international conflicts might be solved through negotiation and economic sanctions more often than through war.

If women were the decision makers, a downside would be a complaint from men and women about there being too much talk and not enough action; call it the "yada, yada, yada" objection. However, with enough time, there might be a replacement of that male bias towards solving problems with arms and violence (Iraq, Afghanistan, Iran, etc.) to solve world problems. This would take generations of experience to bring about, but it is possible.

The ancient Minoan culture on the island to Crete was non-violent, the diet was plant-based (no meat), and it men and women shared power equally. Their deity was a woman with a son, as they believed women's power to create new life, albeit with a man's help was supernatural! Most people assume war has always been with us, but the existence of this culture before the rise of the ancient Greek classical culture, proves this wrong. The balance changed dramatically when iron was introduced from cultures north of Greece and killing animals for food and enemies for revenge/protection became common.

Would it be possible for women to rule indefinitely and eventually eliminate men's bias toward immediate and forceful, deadly reaction to a threat? It would take a great deal of emphasis on redirecting that energy, replacing it with joys in seeing people live whole lives, and less appeal from guns and explosives (I cringe when I see young kids and their video games full of global destruction and body-destroying mayhem)! The current emphasis on husbands and fathers playing a stronger role in their children's care, education, and development is a strong trend toward this healthy redirection.

This I know for sure: If women ruled the world, there would not be the current national debate about contraception. Instead, the talk would be about the new, safe, effective male contraceptive methods now available to all who wanted them!

(Estelle Ford-Williamson, instructor)

SURVEY #13

There would be a broader, more acceptable view of what is beautiful when it comes to the physical attributes of women. There wouldn't be so much focus on our bodies but more of who we are inside. The world wouldn't be so hypersexual. The term "sex sells" wouldn't be a main selling point, especially in the entertainment industry. There wouldn't be wars. Women like to talk and reason to come to a solution. I think the world would be fairer. We think of others before ourselves. We would take better care of each other as a human race.

We are already "Mothers" of the world. So I think we would see more nurturing. Unfortunately if this happened, we would be out of God's order. When we are not in line with God's order then there will be more problems. According to His words we are the male's helpmate. I think as a help mate we will see more results because this is God's order.

No matter how powerful a "power-saw" is, it won't function without the help of a power socket. We are the power socket. God made us that way. Every powerful man has a "power-socket" (wife) that he plugs into.

(Tatiana and Marilyn Paisley, Granddaughter and Daughter of Violet Mitchell)

SURVEYS BY MEN

Written In Their Own Words

5 Surveys

SURVEY #1

If women ruled the world we would not be as advanced scientifically as we are now. Which may not be a bad thing?

There may be fewer wars, because women negotiate better.

Many pleasures men indulge in (may/could) be a thing of the past, i.e.: Playboy X-rated movies, girlie shows…

A good thing may be better politicians. (There are more honest ladies than men.)

Racisms and intolerance may (?) be eradicated.

Boxing will be abolished

NASCAR may be lost in the shuffle.

Criminals will get stiffer terms and serve them. (No more I found God).

Miss America pageant may be abolished.

I have a hundred more. Next time you ask I will give them.

Good luck in your quest.

(Dr. C. H. Smith)

SURVEY #2

There would be less crime, more compassion. Decisions would change more frequently. Pro-abortion nationwide. Neutralization pay. Extended leave after birth. Schools would have (?) of makes required.

The added criticism is all part of your journey. There will be positives in it also.

(No Name)

SURVEY #3

Not much! Women can be as ruthless as men, if not more.

(No Name)

SURVEY #4

Ways of thinking, feeling, and emotions overall.

(No Name)

SURVEY #5

Family would be more important than anything. Work policy in regards to family and vacations or time off would be more flexible. The pay for women would be the same as men.

A mother would be well respected in the work place. Children or childhood would last a lot longer. Math would not be a required subject...it would be incorporated in other subjects. Voting would be more flexible...probably on weekends. When bathrooms are built, there will be more for women than men or at least 2 or 3 times larger than the men's bathroom. Sports would not interfere with anything. Less meetings and a lot more actual work getting done. Stay-at-home moms would be paid... and it would be against the law to separate mothers from their children. There would finally be world peace.

(Gerald M. Powell)

CLOSING STATEMENT

CLOSING STATEMENT
By Shelley J. Taylor

I'm so glad to finish my assignment; I know it will be a *controversial* subject. It was not by my might to write these words, but by the Almighty. Only men and women who do unspeakable crimes mentioned will be labeled, and afflicted with the *Mark of the Beast,* otherwise life goes on in all the traditional ways men have. What you do in the dark is between you and God, as long as it does not go against any of the crimes mentioned. Men will not lose their position as men; most men are good God-fearing men, no doubt.

I can't apologize for anything that might offend anyone because I'm just the messenger. To be honest with you, I prefer to write stories of fiction, but this message has haunted me for over three years. Change will come in several generations or in several millenniums, I don't know. Keep your eyes opened because it is happening—little by little, bit by bit, inch by inch.

There is a lot of work to be done by women to turn this hurting world into the creation God intended for it to be. I must mention the female infanticide (the killing of female babies or fetus). This practice goes on primarily in India, China and Nepal. The murder of the newborn is usually by smothering, drowning, starvation, or poisoning. Female infanticide has been in existence for centuries. Do you think the killings of just female babies were established by women? Probably Not!

Before I end this discussion, I just want to say a few words about the horrible destruction of genocide in Rwanda in 1994. Close to one million people were killed in a matter of one hundred days. The sexual assault on women and children are just too painful for me to write about. So you see, around the world, before women can take their place to rule, all women will have to be on board. *It can happen, and it will happen.* **When Women Rule the World…What Would Change?**